garden of truth

RUTH CHOU SIMONS

BESTSELLING AUTHOR OF *gracelaced*

HARVEST HOUSE PUBLISHERS
EUGENE, OREGON

Cover by Nicole Dougherty

Interior design by Janelle Coury

Published in association with William K. Jensen Literary Agency, 119 Bampton Court, Eugene, Oregon 97404.

GARDEN OF TRUTH

Copyright © 2018 Ruth Chou Simons
Published by Harvest House Publishers
Eugene, Oregon 97408
www.harvesthousepublishers.com

ISBN 978-0-7369-6908-6 (pbk.)

Printed in China

18 19 20 21 22 23 24 25 26 / RDS-JC / 10 9 8 7 6 5 4 3 2

Dear friend,

You may not have a green thumb or consider yourself a natural gardener, but spiritually you are sowing and growing each day through the thoughts that inform your mind and direct your heart. More than simple platitudes or self-help clichés, the words of the Bible transform because they both reveal and restore, cut and console. To trust in the truths of Scripture is to sow wisely. We can choose to listen either to ourselves in the day-to-day or to the faithful Word of God. Preaching truth to ourselves reminds our souls, through God's Word, who the Master Gardener is and what He is cultivating in the soil of our lives through the hope of the gospel.

These 58 verses and accompanying applications serve as seeds to sow in the garden of truth God is cultivating in you. I pray these small beginnings take root, grow into a deeper knowledge of His Word, and bloom into a greater love for His story in you.

Because of grace,

Ruth

...if anyone is in Christ, he is a new creation...

You've been created for
a renewing of the mind,
a transformation of the heart,
and an opening of the eyes to
see where life comes from.
Nothing but Christ will satisfy because
you've been created to be alive in Him.

If anyone is in Christ, he is a new creation.
The old has passed away;
behold, the new has come.

2 CORINTHIANS 5:17

...his mercies never come
to an end...

When opportunities, patience,
comforts, and sometimes
even relationships come to their end,
we can hope in this:
God's love and mercy do not run out.
His well does not run dry,
and His love never grows cold.

The steadfast love of the LORD never ceases;
his mercies never come to an end;
they are new every morning;
great is your faithfulness.

LAMENTATIONS 3:22-23

...by grace you have been saved...

Any good works we produce spring
from the cross at work in us.
So lay down your pride and your striving;
receive, instead, the gift of grace
that enables us to walk by faith.

By grace you have been saved through faith.
And this is not your own doing;
it is the gift of God.

EPHESIANS 2:8

...your steadfast love is better than life, my lips will praise you...

If we become what we behold,
the life of praise we want to live
begins with setting our hearts on
the greatness and
steadfast love of our Savior.

I have looked upon you in the sanctuary,
beholding your power and glory.
Because your steadfast love is better than life,
my lips will praise you.
So I will bless you as long as I live;
in your name I will lift up my hands.

PSALM 63:2-4

...apart from me you can do nothing...

We long for showy fruit when
the Lord calls us to focus on clinging to Him.
We want to produce, but He reminds us that
He provides as we abide.
Abiding is not inactive.

I am the vine; you are the branches.
Whoever abides in me and I in him,
he it is that bears much fruit,
for apart from me you can do nothing.

JOHN 15:5

...in him
my heart
trusts...

...and I am
helped ...

A heart of thanksgiving and praise
chooses to trust in God and hides itself
behind His shield of strength.

The LORD is my strength and my shield;
in him my heart trusts, and I am helped;
my heart exults, and with my song
I give thanks to him.

PSALM 28:7

...set your minds on minds on things that are above...

It's natural to think continually of our earthly
circumstances and possessions,
but we are no longer bound to what comes
naturally because we are hidden in Christ.
Now we can set our minds on eternal things.

If then you have been raised with Christ,
seek the things that are above, where Christ is,
seated at the right hand of God.
Set your minds on things that are above,
not on things that are on earth.
For you have died, and your life is
hidden with Christ in God.

COLOSSIANS 3:1-3

...fear not, for I am
with you...

That a holy, sovereign, good God is
with us is our greatest confidence,
assurance, and strength.
We have nothing to fear when our
God promises to be near.

Fear not, for I am with you; be not dismayed,
for I am your God; I will strengthen you,
I will help you, I will uphold you with
my righteous right hand.

ISAIAH 41:10

...he will
sustain
you...

Are you worn out from controlling and
keeping all things afloat?
You weren't made to
carry everything on your own.

Cast your burden on the Lord,
and he will sustain you;
he will never permit the righteous to be moved.

PSALM 55:22

...we are his workmanship, created in Christ Jesus for good works...

The one truth that casts out all insecurity and doubt:
We are lovingly created by Him and for Him.
He makes no mistakes in His workmanship.
He's created and enabled you for exactly
what He's called you to do.

We are his workmanship,
created in Christ Jesus for good works,
which God prepared beforehand,
that we should walk in them.

EPHESIANS 2:10

...give thanks in all circumstances...

Chances are your "all circumstances"
are not ones you planned on.
But finding God's will in them is
less complicated than you might think this day.
To rejoice always, pray continually,
and give thanks right where you are
is God's will for you...found.

Rejoice always, pray without ceasing,
give thanks in all circumstances;
for this is the will of God in Christ Jesus for you.

1 THESSALONIANS 5:16-18

...let us draw
near with a
true heart in
full assurance
of faith...

Because the blood of Christ purchased the torn veil, the open door, and the welcome mat, we don't stay away in guilt or fear. We come, falling on His grace and grateful to have the assurance that we are not strangers but sons and daughters who may draw near.

Therefore, brothers, since we have confidence to
enter the holy places by the blood of Jesus,
by the new and living way that he opened for us
through the curtain, that is, through his flesh,
and since we have a great priest over the house of God,
let us draw near with a true heart in full assurance of faith,
with our hearts sprinkled clean from
an evil conscience and our bodies
washed with pure water.

HEBREWS 10:19-22

...there is therefore now no condemnation...

What wonder it is that
everything that condemns us
has been nailed to the cross and
paid for by Christ's blood.
If He declares us righteous and spoken for,
let us not say otherwise.

There is therefore now
no condemnation for those who
are in Christ Jesus.

ROMANS 8:1

... in due season
we will reap ...

In due season...
the around-the-corner we can't see and
sometimes struggle to believe.
But because the harvest is the Lord's, not ours,
we can press on in faith,
knowing that He not only sustains
but spurs us on in His service.

And let us not grow weary of doing good,
for in due season we will reap,
if we do not give up.

GALATIANS 6:9

... breathed out
by god ...

When we don't know where to turn,
we remember: God's Word is alive,
it's effective, and it's the place we must turn to
for the transformation we need.

All Scripture is breathed out by God and
profitable for teaching, for reproof,
for correction, and for training in righteousness.

2 TIMOTHY 3:16

...the lifter of my head...

Our God not only stands guard
over our hearts, He lifts our eyes
that we might see Him and His glory
when we don't have the strength
to look up on our own.

You, O LORD, are a shield about me,
my glory, and the lifter of my head.

PSALM 3:3

...power is made
perfect in
weakness...

It's backward but true:
What we need is not better
strategy or greater drive.
What we need is a truer view of our own
weakness and a coming to the end of ourselves.
God calls the end of our try-in-our-own-strength
the beginning of His stand-back-and-watch-Me.

But he said to me,
"My grace is sufficient for you,
for my power is made perfect in weakness."
Therefore I will boast all the more gladly
of my weaknesses,
so that the power of Christ
may rest upon me.

2 CORINTHIANS 12:9

...only God who gives
the growth...

Maybe you're cultivating,
maybe you're watering,
or maybe you're waiting for breakthrough.
Don't try to rush the process, and don't give up.
Our Father alone causes your garden to grow.

So neither he who plants
nor he who waters is anything,
but only God who gives the growth.

1 CORINTHIANS 3:7

... but
you have received
the Spirit of adoption
as sons...

Knowing we are beloved children
changes everything.
We're wanted, chosen,
and welcomed by a loving Father.

For you did not receive the spirit of slavery to
fall back into fear, but you have received
the Spirit of adoption as sons,
by whom we cry, "Abba! Father!"

ROMANS 8:15

...he who is in you
is greater...

As we hide ourselves in Him,
He who is greater than all that presses in
around us keeps us safe and
secure in His care.

Little children, you are from God and
have overcome them, for he who is in you
is greater than he who is in the world.

1 JOHN 4:4

... you were bought
with a price ...

When you look into the mirror and
struggle to see worth,
take God at His Word and act accordingly:
You are a conduit of grace,
a vessel of worship—redeemed to
reflect the treasure of Christ in you.

Do you not know that your body is
a temple of the Holy Spirit within you,
whom you have from God?
You are not your own,
for you were bought with a price.
So glorify God in your body.

1 CORINTHIANS 6:19-20

...God made alive together with him...

When you're tempted to pick up that
heavy load of shame and guilt, remember:
He canceled your debt on the cross;
you are no longer guilty, condemned,
and enslaved.

And you,
who were dead in your trespasses and
the uncircumcision of your flesh,
God made alive together with him,
having forgiven us all our trespasses,
by canceling the record of debt that
stood against us with its legal demands.
This he set aside, nailing it to the cross.

COLOSSIANS 2:13-14

... I am the Lord who practices steadfast love ...

At the end of the day, we can possess nothing
greater than communion with a holy God.
We were created for relationship with Him.
Nothing else will satisfy.

Let him who boasts boast in this,
that he understands and knows me,
that I am the LORD who practices steadfast love,
justice, and righteousness in the earth.
For in these things I delight, declares the LORD.

JEREMIAH 9:24

...God is our refuge
and strength ...

He is, in this very moment,
our help and our hope.
Why do we seek refuge elsewhere
when He is at the ready?

God is our refuge and strength,
a very present help in trouble.

PSALM 46:1

... but seek first the kingdom of God ...

Whether finances, health, family, or personal concerns, our worries and anxieties subside when we turn our minds to God's provision we don't deserve, His kindness we rarely see coming, His Word that satisfies beyond our hunger, and His sovereignty we don't realize is so much wiser than our own.

Therefore do not be anxious, saying,
"What shall we eat?" or
"What shall we drink?" or "What shall we wear?"
For the Gentiles seek after all these things,
and your heavenly Father knows that you need them all.
But seek first the kingdom of God and his righteousness,
and all these things will be added to you.

MATTHEW 6:31-33

...the Lord
looks on the
heart...

More than anything,
we need to learn to see our circumstances
and ourselves as God sees them.
When we deem worthy what He calls worthy,
that's when we begin to know what
the Lord considers truly beautiful.

But the LORD said to Samuel,
"Do not look on his appearance or
on the height of his stature,
because I have rejected him.
For the LORD sees not as man sees:
man looks on the outward appearance,
but the LORD looks on the heart."

1 SAMUEL 16:7

...my Redeemer lives...

The simple truth that
we must remember today is that
our Redeemer isn't a fairy tale or
a moment in history;
He is alive and at work now and
will complete what He has begun.

For I know that my Redeemer lives,
and at the last he will stand upon the earth.

JOB 19:25

... be found to result
in praise and glory
and honor
at the revelation of
Jesus Christ...

It's not wasted, friend—this trial, this suffering,
this fire you're going through.
The Lord promises purpose in all of it,
for the purifying of your faith and the praise of
His name when you see His faithfulness through it.

In this you rejoice, though now for a little while,
if necessary, you have been grieved by various trials,
so that the tested genuineness of your faith—
more precious than gold that perishes
though it is tested by fire—
may be found to result in praise and glory and
honor at the revelation of Jesus Christ.

1 PETER 1:6-7

...walk in
newness of life ...

Don't keep looking to the past,
revisiting again and again
the guilt you once knew.
When Jesus declares us new,
we are no longer who we were before.
Walk in it by believing what He says about you.

We were buried therefore with him
by baptism into death,
in order that, just as Christ was raised from
the dead by the glory of the Father,
we too might walk in newness of life.

ROMANS 6:4

...blessed
is the man
who
remains
steadfast
under
trial...

How do we remain steadfast?
Certainly not by our own might or strategy.
Our only hope is to anchor ourselves to
the steadfastness of God,
who calls us to abide in Him.

Blessed is the man who
remains steadfast under trial,
for when he has stood the test
he will receive the crown of life,
which God has promised
to those who love him.

JAMES 1:12

... Christ died for us ...

Whatever failures you are mentally rehearsing
today can no longer keep you at
arm's length from His love...so let them go.
God sought you out and made you His own
while you were unlovely.
It is He who redeems and makes you worthy.

God shows his love for us
in that while we were still sinners,
Christ died for us.

ROMANS 5:8

...that in me
you may have
peace...

We know who wins in the end—
the One who has already overcome our hearts.
The suffering and trials we face today in
this broken world are not the end of the story...
wait upon Him who makes all things new.

I have said these things to you,
that in me you may have peace.
In the world you will have tribulation.
But take heart; I have overcome the world.

JOHN 16:33

... I live by faith ...

How freeing it is when we realize
we can stop trying to prove ourselves to
other people through achievement and effort.
Our lives are not our own!

I have been crucified with Christ.
It is no longer I who live,
but Christ who lives in me.
And the life I now live in the flesh
I live by faith in the Son of God,
who loved me and gave himself for me.

GALATIANS 2:20

...your word is truth...

Something will shape us and
form us into who we become—
it can either be the truth of God's Word
or our own feelings.
Let it be His truth that transforms us.

Sanctify them in the truth;
your word is truth.

JOHN 17:17

... a day in
your courts is
better than a thousand
elsewhere ...

We can run to fun, family, friends,
and even fashion to fill us up,
but the psalmist knows:
No other place but in
God's presence will truly satisfy.

For a day in your courts is better than
a thousand elsewhere.
I would rather be a doorkeeper
in the house of my God
than dwell in the tents of wickedness.

PSALM 84:10

...do not be anxious about anything...

As we pray and give thanks for
what God has done, we remember that,
because He has already brought us
to Himself through the cross,
there is no place, no circumstance,
and no future to which He cannot bring peace.

Do not be anxious about anything,
but in everything by prayer and
supplication with thanksgiving let your requests
be made known to God.
And the peace of God,
which surpasses all understanding,
will guard your hearts and your minds
in Christ Jesus.

PHILIPPIANS 4:6-7

...nor anything else
in all creation,
will be able to
separate us from
the love of God...

Nothing—
not even the lies we make up about ourselves—
can keep us from God's love for us. Friend,
His love is strong...
and it has traversed heaven and earth for you.

For I am sure that neither death nor life,
nor angels nor rulers, nor things present nor things
to come, nor powers, nor height nor depth,
nor anything else in all creation,
will be able to separate us from
the love of God in Christ Jesus our Lord.

ROMANS 8:38-39

...his
faithfulness
will be
your shield...

The siege may be from without or within,
but we've not been left vulnerable or exposed.
Mighty yet tender...God is both our fortified wall
of defense and our soft covering.
That is our faithful Lord.

He will cover you with his feathers,
and under his wings you will find refuge;
his faithfulness will be your shield and rampart.

PSALM 91:4 (NIV)

...stay alert
and
be clearheaded...

This world and its distractions and
allure will lull us to complacency if we let it.
We are just passing through, friend.
Stay awake and keep your eyes open...
this is not our home.

So be on your guard,
not asleep like the others.
Stay alert and be clearheaded.

1 THESSALONIANS 5:6 (NLT)

... we have
this treasure in
jars of clay...

We may be worn, average,
unimpressive vessels.
But let it be so—
the true treasure is the gospel in us.

But we have this treasure in jars of clay,
to show that the surpassing power belongs
to God and not to us.

2 CORINTHIANS 4:7

...the joy
of the Lord is
your strength...

The truth of God's Word explained and treasured (as with Israel!) brings relief and joy to a weary, grieving soul.
Why do we turn to anything else?
No distraction, fix, frivolity, or formula will provide what the balm of truth can.

...This day is holy to our LORD.
And do not be grieved,
for the joy of the Lord is your strength.

NEHEMIAH 8:10

... he who began
a good work
in you will
bring it to
completion ...

You are a work in progress.
What defines you is not what you
will accomplish in a lifetime but what
God will complete in you
as you hide your life in His.

I am sure of this,
that he who began a good work in you
will bring it to completion
at the day of Jesus Christ.

PHILIPPIANS 1:6

... I am fearfully and wonderfully made ...

No one knows us better than the Lord.
All those things we appreciate about ourselves—
and all that we struggle to embrace—
He purposefully made in us to bring Him glory.

For you formed my inward parts;
you knitted me together in my mother's womb.
I praise you, for I am fearfully and
wonderfully made.

PSALM 139:13-14

... there is
one mediator
between
God and men...

Christ stands in the gap for us—
in the chasm of fear, guilt, and unholiness—
and calls us His and acceptable before God.
No matter where you've been or where
your thoughts have taken you today,
Jesus swings wide the door to
God's presence through His blood.

There is one God,
and there is one mediator
between God and men,
the man Christ Jesus.

1 TIMOTHY 2:5

... he will
lift
you up...

Give up on trying to
make much of yourself, friend.
That acknowledgment you seek and
that respect you long for
finds its true fulfillment in the honor God gives
to a heart that bows before Him.

Humble yourselves before the Lord,
and he will lift you up.

JAMES 4:10 (NIV)

...keep yourselves
in the
love of God...

Keep thinking on God's love,
keep meditating on His Word,
keep putting away striving,
and wait upon the Lord.
His love fuels our perseverance.

But you, beloved, building yourselves up in
your most holy faith and praying in the Holy Spirit,
keep yourselves in the love of God,
waiting for the mercy of our Lord Jesus Christ
that leads to eternal life.

JUDE 1:20-21

... as far as
the east is from
the west...

We are more loved and forgiven
than we willingly accept.
Why live as condemned and rejected
when Jesus crossed immeasurable distances
to secure forgiveness for us?

For as high as the heavens are above the earth,
so great is his steadfast love
toward those who fear him;
as far as the east is from the west,
so far does he remove our transgressions from us.

PSALM 103:11-12

...we are the
aroma
of Christ...

Walk among the lilies,
and you will carry the fragrance of lilies.
Walk in Christ, and you will release
the aroma of Him who saves.
Stay so close that the fragrance of
His grace may linger wherever you go.

For we are the aroma of Christ to God
among those who are being saved and
among those who are perishing,

2 CORINTHIANS 2:15

... whose mind
is stayed on you...

Cling to what is true:
Peace follows trust,
and trust is found in the place
we fix our eyes and set our hearts.
Let that place be You, Lord.

You keep him in perfect peace
whose mind is stayed on you,
because he trusts in you.

ISAIAH 26:3

... rested from his works ...

Friend, cutting corners on rest
doesn't get you ahead.
You were made to rest, and rest in Him.

Whoever has entered God's rest
has also rested from his works
as God did from his.

HEBREWS 4:10

...to obey is better than sacrifice...

All that amazing stuff we do for the Lord
that keeps us running around and frazzled?
What if He's not impressed with
how much we accomplish for Him
but how much we are willing to listen to Him?
Consider how the Lord might be asking you
to listen and obey today.

Has the LORD as great delight in
burnt offerings and sacrifices,
as in obeying the voice of the LORD?
Behold, to obey is better than sacrifice,
and to listen than the fat of rams.

1 SAMUEL 15:22

...beauty for ashes...

Our circumstances may not turn
around in an instant,
but the condition of our hearts can—
when God replaces our despair
with the joy of His salvation.

To all who mourn in Israel,
he will give a crown of beauty for ashes,
a joyous blessing instead of mourning,
festive praise instead of despair.
In their righteousness, they will be like
great oaks that the LORD has planted
for his own glory.

ISAIAH 61:3 (NLT)

... our
citizenship
is in
heaven ...

We were made for another world;
we needn't be surprised when we find that
we just don't belong here,
when we find ourselves yearning
for our true home.

But our citizenship is in heaven,
and from it we await a Savior,
the Lord Jesus Christ.

PHILIPPIANS 3:20

...behold,
I am making
all things
new...

When your weary bones, tired feet,
and broken heart feel like giving up,
remember that God is—at this very minute—
preparing for your future with Him,
where He will make all things new,
and everything sad comes untrue (Tolkein).

"He will wipe away every tear from their eyes,
and death shall be no more,
neither shall there be mourning,
nor crying, nor pain anymore,
for the former things have passed away."
And he who was seated on the throne said,
"Behold, I am making all things new."
Also he said, "Write this down,
for these words are trustworthy and true."

REVELATION 21:4-5

... my God
will supply
every need ...

Where we feel lacking in resources,
God fortifies.
Where we feel weak in the fight,
He replenishes.
Where we can't see a way out,
He illuminates the path of life through His Word.
Because we serve a God who owns it all,
His supply never runs out.

My God will supply every need of yours
according to his riches in glory in Christ Jesus.

PHILIPPIANS 4:19

...He gives us
the victory...

Sometimes we forget that the battle—
the conquering of alienation for the
place of welcome at the throne of God—
is already won in Christ.
What have we to lose when He's
claimed victory in what matters most?

But thanks be to God!
He gives us the victory through
our Lord Jesus Christ.

1 CORINTHIANS 15:57 (NIV)

...for the Lord
and not
for men...

Who we look to please today will
determine both our attitude and the outcome.
If we chase the praise of others,
we will never stop running.
If we set our eyes on the prize that is
to come, the energy we need for
today's tasks will be supplied by
the God we look to please.

Whatever you do, work heartily,
as for the Lord and not for men,
knowing that from the Lord you will receive
the inheritance as your reward.
You are serving the Lord Christ.

COLOSSIANS 3:23-24

...possible with god...

Maybe the Lord has allowed a circumstance
that has no quick resolution or a relationship
that feels forever broken
so that you might know that
it is His will and His way that
makes the impossible possible.

Jesus replied,
"What is impossible with man
is possible with God."

LUKE 18:27 (NIV)

MORE BEAUTY AND TRUTH FROM
RUTH CHOU SIMONS...

Become immersed in carefully crafted meditations surrounded by hundreds of pieces of watercolor art in *GraceLaced*: Discovering Timeless Truths through Seasons of the Heart. Featuring handlettered scriptures interwoven with the floral compositions Ruth Simons is known for, *GraceLaced* extends a soul-stirring invitation to draw close to God while...

- *resting* in who He is
- *rehearsing* the truth He says about you
- *responding* in faith to those truths
- *remembering* His provision to sustain you, time and time again

Who we are and *who God is* never changes, though everything else does. Let this book point you to truth as you journey through the changing seasons of your heart.

Ruth Chou Simons is an artist, writer, entrepreneur, and speaker. As creator of the popular GraceLaced online shoppe, blog, and Instagram community, she shares scriptural truths daily through her hand-painted artwork and words. Ruth and her husband, Troy, live in New Mexico and are grateful parents to six sons—their greatest adventure.